Excitations of Entanglement

Also by John Bartlett and published by Ginninderra Press
Awake at 3 a.m.
Eschatology (Pocket Poets)
This Luminous Earth (Pocket Poets)

John Bartlett

Excitations of Entanglement

Excitations of Entanglement
ISBN 978 1 76109 613 6
Copyright © text John Bartlett 2023
Cover image: Ryutaro Tsukata from Pexels

First published 2023 by
GINNINDERRA PRESS
PO Box 3461 Port Adelaide 5015
www.ginninderrapress.com.au

Contents

Preface	9
Ashes to Ashes	11
These Savage Mysteries	13
Holding the Hurt	15
Are we there yet?	16
Will memories be enough?	18
Swallowing the Ocean	20
A time to clear stones away	21
In vacated spaces	23
Cetacean Stranding	24
The Waxing of the Gibbous Moon	25
Measuring	27
These Days	28
Days of Broken Glass	30
Some 21st Century Compositions	31
Avian Behaviours	32
The Beginnings of Sorrows	33
An Orange	34
Downloading Reality	35
Some Assumptions	36
Stay Quietly in Your Seats	37
Lizard	39
I Am Not a Sex Doll	40
That River	41
Aged 12, or Thereabouts	42
Portia Faces Life	43
So Much	44
Hieroglyphs of Breath	45
No Peace Without Bitterness	47

Ekaterinburg	49
Glenside Hospital, 1956	50
Now Wake the Prowling Tigers	52
Installations	53
Hey Bro, posting your hard-ons on Twitter won't stop Global Warming	55
Go Firmly	58
That Hereness/Thereness Thing	59
The Taste of the Wolf	61
Those Vows of Silence	62
Outside IGA	63
Ballast	64
Afternoons	65
Michelangelo's Failure	66
To Be Wild	67
Passer, deliciae	68
This Corner	69
The Carnage of Petals	70
Full-throated	71
The Elastic Horizon	72
Falling	73
To Have Some Weight	75
A Box of Photos	76
living with erasures	77
investigate	78
pilgrimages of the short-finned eel	79
Latitude 38 South	80
languages of hands	81
The Calling	82
A DNA test	83
Nevinbumbaan Returns	85
these bodies of men	86

Still 'Falling'	87
All the Deep Pulse	88
ice creams and AK47s	89
open waters	91
In No Particular Order	92
the road to Ronda	93
westerlies	95
Waiting	96
Rioting on the Equinox	97
sunflowers need full sunshine	98
Waiting for light	99
Let the bright Seraphim	100
Arias of Longing	102
Communion	103
Sing Out for Ukraine	104
shall be changed	106
Anthem for a Redeeming Youth	108
after all kinds of walking around	109
Acknowlegements	111
About the author	112

Preface

Excitations of entanglement, a process taken from nuclear physics, is a perfect metaphor for this poetry of encounter with people, with nature, with memory and the landscapes of the imagination. The process describes the way some atomic particles can become entangled by various excitation processes, locked together even if they are separated. The effect is mostly brief, sometimes only microseconds.

The best-known demonstration relates to photon entanglement, where light particles become entangled and share a relationship such that if something happens to one the other is affected even if they are a significant distance apart.

The business of achieving entanglement is the excitation process.

The state of the planet has heightened our own individual and community excitations locked us together in a common humanity, sometimes only briefly or separated and isolated from each other too. Unexpectedly we became entangled in each other's lives, sharing common tragedies.

Here is a collection of poetry reacting to contemporary influences, whether it's by fire, the ocean or by birds as auguries of a spiritual reality waiting to be revealed.

Here we meet humans often at their worst, as uncontrollable and vengeful mobs but also with individuals who leave indelible marks on us, that can be both erotic as well as spiritual. We are entangled with each other and changed forever.

Ashes to Ashes

when parrots plunge songless
to scorched earth
when screams in burning treetops
turn our sleep to static
when weeping men
face oceans of fire,
continents shift,
we become the running dead,
hope-stripped, scorched,
and hollowed out,
charred at the edges of
our dreams, flayed by fire and loss, we
breathe in the smoky atoms
of incinerated creatures,
transformed into the totems
of what's been lost,
we are now the Elements,
the spirits wrought from
earth and air, from
fire and water, sentenced
to carry our scorched souls
like excess baggage,
pilgrims in unfamiliar
bushlands, roaming, searching
for some kind of hope.

Why else do we scatter wide
the ashes of our beloveds
if not for a
holy communion,
lest we be condemned to
the dungeons of ourselves?

These Savage Mysteries

after Romans 8:38–39

In 1962 I failed Physics 101
       – stunned by the uncertainty principle
I puzzle still this pulsing mass
this compulsion of atoms
into which we're thrust.

When I hear the wind in Moonah tops
my mind takes flight
joins these particles in
their cosmic ratatouille.

If seen by none,
is a tree still a tree, does it
exist without my gaze?

does each wave subsume itself
in the roiling sea's melange
withholding personal ambitions?

where do they go, those waves,
that swell, that ripple out
from swans' carouse?

All these questions of the universe
stitched together into a coverlet
of brilliant constellations, galaxies
where none can see the seams

where nothing separates us, neither death
nor life, nor angels, nor powers
nor things past or to come.

Nothing can separate us
from this ocean's flow,
this back and forth
these invisible waves,
these fields of ghosts,
this world of molecules

expanding into birth,
       – too late now to gather up
these savage mysteries

Oh you quantum physicists,
you theologians disguised
in lab-coat drag,
who priest us into
excitations of
entanglement.

Holding the Hurt

In the ruins of the burnt-out home
he finds enough rope
to fashion a noose, till the dog
nudges his legs, time for a walk

Scratching the ashes, she searches
for her grandmother's rings,
finds one photo album
completely unburnt

His life concertinaed to
six plastic bags in
the back of his ute
he holds his hurt to his chest
like a stillborn child

Are we there yet?

It is not possible for the bad or the good to endure forever –
Cervantes in *Don Quixote*

'All we have is now'
according to my shirt label
        – was this good or bad news
and – hadn't that 'now' already vanished?

breakfast cereals too were delivering
messages determinedly evangelical
'we believe in wholesome goodness'
        – epigrams, maxims and aphorisms
        (even sermons)
were erupting overnight
like unexplainable cold sores
        – harbingers all
like the cormorants busy drying their
funereal wings and isn't that Satan I see
doing deals on his mobile
walking up and down the empty spaces?

        – so masked and sanitised to the bone
we must tread the earth differently now,
reverently – like reclusive red hermit crabs,
our eye-stalks flattened by addiction to
counting curving charts, as we
protect our soft underbellies
from rumours of indefinite detention

who guards the emergency codes
that we need to pause this
daily download of bodies to our hard drive?

CAUTION –
PLEASE ADJUST your own mask before
stampeding towards the emergency chute

Will memories be enough?

It's called the Unsettlement
a time of empty spaces,
– we dwell in corrugated
air awaiting rain

ringing hollow, when tapped
        – we've all been here before
in those gaps simmering
with alarm – a lover leaving

slams a door, no back-looking
        – so who now owns these streets?
aren't they the ghosts of
promises so far unfulfilled?

what (or who) will carry us across
this Uncanny?
        – must I trawl through
memory for a remedy, like

        – first entering Manila Bay
        – stepping onto New York streets
        – entering the Mesquita in Cordoba,
feeling my soul fly up or

        – watching snow cloak the
        Burghers of Calais in Washington
        – riding trams in Bourke Street
dazzled by your always?

Will this thin membrane of
my memories stretch, or
be strong enough to carry us
away from the disappointment

that we are merely human?
        – be a bridge to the other
lives that wait, like explorers,
nameless & impatient?

Swallowing the Ocean

for Behrouz Boochani

and when the earth fell away
below us (where once was strong)
our Coming From was gone, our
Going To, unknown

our lives then, small enough
to hold inside cupped hands,
for close inspection, – we,
guarded by the not-angels,
processed like fakes, using
our no-names, under the heat
of that foreign sun, *scavenging
for scraps of light*, for some Nows,
stripped of our skins
layer by layer, our
anonymous bones exposed,
bartering for more time

– so must I interrogate the ocean,
saying, 'shall I swallow you
again until I choke on your
mendacious horizon?'

       – because here in this Great
Southern Land they still
fail to notice what a change of wind
means on a looming fire-front

A time to clear stones away

after Ecclesiastes 3:1–8

Uneasily falls the light on empty streets,
our blighted souls between two worlds,
dressed only in the tatters of our plans,
we monitor each other cautiously,
alert for invisible assassins,
we surrender our anonymous dead,
sacrificed without words or flowers,
stacking their coffins high,
Leggo-ed bulwarks against our pain,
                – and yet

magpies still wake us, their
songs are bells of consecration,
creeks still creep seaward with delight,

in deepest forests, trees
still yearn slowly skyward,
the Eastern grey egret, relentless,
fossicks in wetland mud,
all you   prophets of patience,
the Continuum of Love overlaying us yet.

Did we forget to touch our sacred land,
let dreams unfettered fly,
gaze wordless at the moon divine?

remember
to everything there is a season,
a time to every purpose.
This is the time to go within
to find in stillness who we are,
to step aside, allow the earth take charge,
a time to clear away the stones,
await the songs of magpies
yet to be composed.

In vacated spaces

where wolves walked to carry stones
we struggle to stand upright
as Athena dropped a mountain and
all the stars fell down

we struggle to stand upright
while your smile is a loaded gun
all the stars fell down
I may not reach the other side

while your smile is a loaded gun
despatch your genocidal god
I may not reach the other side
unless herons lead to Enlightenment

despatch your genocidal god
wisdom lies where you least expect
unless herons lead to Enlightenment
from the mouths of babes and children

wisdom lies where you least expect
in spaces vacated by the plague
from the mouths of babes and children
where wolves walked to carry stones

Cetacean Stranding

nobody knows why you do it
this full-throttled intent
to beach, this premature step
in evolution from sea to land

did your leaders lure you here
with silky promises of
squid and cod, then
leave you floundering in
the shallows of their deceit?

or did you hear the cries
a child might make at night
to draw you here, despite
low tides and radar warning?

or did sonar static,
like onset dementia confuse,
till kamikaze-like & shore-blown
by anonymous wind divine
you flatlined,
adrift on terra firma?

Your bulk and burden
too heavy for our hearts
                to bear

The Waxing of the Gibbous Moon

inspired by a line from 'Do Not Go Gentle Into That Good Night',
Dylan Thomas

this is the time of
the waxing of the gibbous moon,
suspended at that still point
                between
late afternoon   &   not-yet-twilight
                between
weak-tea sunlight   seesawing with   pale humpbacked
moonlight
in that pre-twilight with its
scattering of wrens
                balanced between
malice   &   full-heartness.

So where are the wild men
who caught and sang the sun in flight
who beat swords into ploughshares,
crafted spears into
fine surgical instruments,
who hammered the long-range missiles
into harmless street installations
where children could climb and play,
men who hurled paper-plane haiku
into the chambers of parliaments,
poked their sonnets into the spokes of despots,
sang their love-song ghazals
in the aisles of supermarkets?

Where are the raging men who
snatched fire from the gods to
backburn for peace,
Where are the men to ensnare
this elusive sun
before the darkness falls?
     Where are you now?

Measuring

I'm in the kitchen, mixing dough
for bread, without a way to measure out

the flour, the milk, one egg or two
how will I know the way

to measure the unknown?
they say that there's

a promising trend, flattening the curve
but the man in the shiny suit

with a wide, red tie
touches the screen and magically,

the graph rises like a 747
but that's in America and Italy

so we must be winning
how good is Australia

but what's the competition
and how do you win?

how do you measure
the weight of a human soul

if the ashes of a cremated life
weigh the same as a newborn baby?

These Days

These days
in the penumbra
of this semi-permanent eclipse
of light
butcher birds surrender
their songs, go home to
roost, wait out this
artificial night

These days pirates
in Dolce & Gabbana suits
have highjacked the halls
of power

Rapists from the suburbs
take oaths of office
on mildewed bibles
these days

These days men
with iPad eyes
stalk the S & P 500
doing deals in arms
while texting 'thoughts & prayers'
to families of children
eviscerated by IUDs

These days
all we like sheep
have gone astray

Will we live to see
the tumbrils of karma
rumble,
crowds shouting
'burn, motherfuckers, burn'?

Will we ever emerge again
to see the stars?

Days of Broken Glass

Why are these days so full of broken glass (wasn't *Kristallnacht* enough?) a helicopter rising treacherous from a hospital helipad, sainted engorged dragonfly filling up an angry sky, oh why an Audi A8 burnt out on the highway to Lifestyle Opportunity near a boy hitchhiking with surfboard *bring out your unbelievers* let them abseil the walls of QAnon, why do the branches of the pear tree tremble so when pigeons touch down lightly and if we follow the white rabbit will it lead to the elite Satan-worshipping paedophiles, *blessed are you if you mourn*, let the army of the aged cry out in the streets for bread and dreams, *let them inherit the earth*, for only the persistence of our blessed memories will *save us from this Abyss* of the Bargain Basement.

Some 21st Century Compositions

Sonata in High C for Whipper Snipper
Duet for Yamaha 1000 and Dump truck
Concerto for two Jet Skis
Rondo for coffee machine
Trio for leaf blower, Whipper Snipper and lawnmower
Opera for a Qantas A380 take-off
Prelude to the Afternoon of a Leaf Blower
Single voice conversation for smartphone on public transport
Duet for barking Dogs

Avian Behaviours

why do magpies walk when
they could fly – are they
just saving fuel or natural
flâneurs, strolling, stickybeaking,
into everybody's business?

why do blackbirds behave like
the crazy uncle at Christmas,
annoying and fidgety
making relatives scatter, like
pieces of unsubstantial mulch?

why do lyrebirds just
perform the cover songs of other birds?
can't they be bothered writing
their own compositions?

and why do kookaburras
just think it's all so
damn funny?

the acrobatic honeyeater
takes her meals
swinging upside down
oblivious to digestion issues

how like us
they really are

The Beginnings of Sorrows

after Matthew 26:6–8

the unravelling cardigans of prime ministers
the fading tattoos of body builders
the tangled earrings of politicians
the falling trousers of stockbrokers
the laddered stockings of major generals
the unmatched socks of parking inspectors
the sagging underpants of property developers
the smudged lipstick of shock jocks
the first wrinkles of porn stars
the jammed zippers of exotic dancers

all these things must come to pass
but the end is not yet

An Orange

In 1735, Italian composer Giovanni Pergolesi
wrote *L'olimpiade*, his final opera. At the Roman premiere
unfortunately, the singers were mediocre, and the audience
hated the music. He had to endure the humiliation of being
struck on the head by an orange hurled by a member of the
audience. A year later he died of consumption at the age of
26. Sorry it's not better news. You will have success
elsewhere...unfortunately not for us

    (a) Thank you for submitting... trusting us with
your work... been handled with care... enjoyed reading
your... appreciate the chance to read... lovely to hear from
you... thank you for thinking of us... we thank you sincerely
for sharing... received many excellent... appreciated the
chance... whilst I'm pleased... whilst we enjoyed this...

    (b) although... we must decline... won't be able...
regret to tell you... sorry to inform you... sorry to
disappoint... unable... some tough selection choices... tough
decisions... have decided to pass... limited in our selection...
decided to pass unfortunately, not for us... unfortunately not
be using it... we won't be accepting any work from you...
unfortunately with such limited space... handful of pieces...
narrow down... won't be able... this time... sorry it's not
better news... unfortunately... you will have success
elsewhere...

Psychoanalysist Sigmund Freud said that the ego is 'like a
man on horseback who has to hold in check the superior
strength of the horse'.
– a rejection notice or an orange to the head is usually
sufficient

Downloading Reality

I've started at last to download reality
From locations not yet googled
My memories are still buffering
Can I cohabit with irrelevance?

From locations not yet googled
Treasures may yet be unearthed
Can I cohabit with irrelevance?
While city noise helps me sleep

Treasures may yet be unearthed
Lights still shine in dark tunnels
While city noise helps me sleep
Decisions are an impossibility

Lights still shine in dark tunnels
Night-vision goggles are sold out
Decisions are an impossibility
The world still waits for a saviour

Night-vision goggles are sold out
Rabbits are digging deeper burrows
The world still waits for a saviour
I've started at last to download reality

Some Assumptions

Women on the way up
may sometimes be forced
to move sideways or
even go through hoops held by men,
though this will be temporary.

Be warned: Do not enter the box
provided by men
elegant as it may appear.

Remember those who ascended
before you, like Mary (the Mother),
despite her job description – 'handmaid',
was assumed by the CEO (of non-binary gender)
straight through the glass ceiling
into Paradise, all intact
(including superannuation)
Who knew all along
'Madonna with Child'
was really
'Resting Bitch Face'?

Stay Quietly in Your Seats

The Romanovs & Ceaușescus
never saw it coming
the Marcoses, waving from the balcony,
mistook the shouts for cheering
until the barricades went down
despots should always keep
a helicopter on standby
in the back garden

In the House of Special Purpose
the Romanovs, bejewelled and bullet-proofed,
shared two chairs,
awaiting further instructions,
royal Martyrs-in-Waiting

When Nicolae on the balcony
told Elena to shut up
we knew it was all over
       – because
when dictators warn restless crowds
'stay quietly in your seats',
Elena shouting out for silence,
the firing squad is drawing straws
for the blank cartridge

While the crowds were tearing down
the barricades in Pennsylvania Avenue
the President was tweeting, calling
to Melania, immobilised, unsure
which dresses could be left behind
forgetting even Imelda (mournful millipede),
abandoned shoes,12,000 pairs

Warning!
When beheading the Hydra
remember
it responds by growing extra heads

Lizard

A lizard runs through the grass
Like a spilled cup of tea
Static crackles from eyried boardrooms
According to the order of Melchisedech

Like a spilled cup of tea
Random thoughts are already tadpoles
According to the order of Melchisedech
While toads are still advancing

Random thoughts are already tadpoles
And some sinners do repent
While toads are still advancing
Climate cannot be denied forever

And some sinners do repent
Though Cardinals wear the colour of blood
Climate cannot be denied forever
As long as brimstone is back in fashion

Though cardinals wear the colour of blood
Lizards favour frilly-collared necks
As long as brimstone is back in fashion
Like a spilled cup of tea

I Am Not a Sex Doll

In China sex dolls are
sashaying off the assembly

lines lip-synching Helen Reddy I
am woman hear me roar

for 1979 and Deng Xiao Ping's one
child decree not enough Made in

China I'm like Travolta just trying to stay
alive stabbing at the box I am not a

robot now that I see songbirds trapped in
forests golden creoles stuck to glue-trap

branch, oh the dread, the tread of
hobnailed men who pit bird

on bird in hellscape's *Who's Got
Talent* but here by the birdbath and

blue-black iris spears a crimson
explosion of parrots proclaims it's

not quite time to break
the emergency glass

how many sex dolls can you see

in your CAPTCHA boxes?

That River

in daylight hours the peacock strutted
vain, coquettish strumpet

on frost-cracked nights his caged cries
disturbed my sleep

while that patient river flowed
through this town and childhood days

with its push and pull and
pulse and throb and flood,

its silver flight of cod in sunlight
its holy waters plumped our gardens

with sweet, black grapes, pomegranate
ripe and red as nipples

its cliffs relinquished ochre stone
to build our church – Redeemer Holy

so mesmerised by incense and
the whiff of sulphur from hellfire threat

I threw myself into those beckoning
baptismal waters, stained by the colour of sin

and let them carry me over snags and
temptations, rescues and redemptions

all the way to the ocean and
the surprise of salt

Aged 12, or Thereabouts

for Wilf Bartlett

when the train to Adelaide
crosses the Millewa river
the steel-taut bridge trembles,
wakes the man in the pylon

under the bridge
waters flow
with rippled violence
hiding sinewey snags,
Mulyewongk alert
for unwitting boys

December 21st, 1912
To honor the heroism
>   of a boy for rescuing
>   from drowning
>   Adam Duncan, aged 12,
>   or thereabouts.

in the flood of '56,
I stood on the bridge
watching ravenous waters
lick the doors of Ridley Mill

this river is not
the Mississippi
or the Amazon
but the river of my childhood
that groans with the pain
of boys becoming men

Portia Faces Life

for Celeste

the brown Bakelite radio
on the shelf near the teapot

tinny voice announcing
'Portia Faces Life'

you dropping mallee roots
into the old wood stove

stirring the bowl, turning the volume
up *for all those in love and*

for all those who can remember then
your apron folded on the green chair back

your footsteps fading in the passageway
my hands reaching into the bowl of

forbiddenness, this small disobedience
moving onto larger disappointments

you said, 'I can't accept you're happier now
but I said, like Portia,

>*I'm just like every woman
>who has ever dared to love*

So Much

after 'Red Wheelbarrow' by William Carlos Williams

So much depends
upon
a red sun
set
to stay or
to go,
upon a black silhouette
in a swan-darkening sky

So much depends
on
the taste of
your kiss
the strength of your touch

So much depends
on how quickly they fade
the photos of you
and that room
of regret
where we last
met

                so much

Hieroglyphs of Breath

I loved you in another country
                with words not mine,
with daylight-textbook phrases,
ako si Juan, taga Australia

      – nights my words on batwing
skittered across rooftops
between us, slipped through the window
of your sleeping room, wrote
secret hieroglyphs on your
naked skin

      – words licked away
our shared bitter spaces
left bloodied handprints like
agnostic stigmata

      – we scanned each other's
bodies, watched
for smiles that might mean
        something (or nothing),
a turn of the head that might
say something else,
      – reduced ourselves to blind semaphores
of hands and flags

how do you
> translate what
> bubbles up from the belly
> of loneliness, roars white-hot
> between the thighs, incinerates
> all resolution
>
> enunciate
> this something that has no other words?

I do remember

paalam mylove paalam means goodbye

No Peace Without Bitterness

At the Fotheringhay Falcon Inn
we order ploughman's lunch,
bread, cheese, pickles
hard-boiled eggs and ale,
unchanged over all these years

At the castle site where
Mary Queen of Scots, in black,
her stockings edged in silver
with green silk gaiters and
petticoats of velvet crimson,
clumsily was beheaded
and later James, her son, in rage
tore down these walls, no stone
remained, this motte alone,
this mound of earth and junk,
its view towards the church
'floating on the hill
above the River Nene, a
galleon of Perpendicular on
a sea of corn'

On the long path to
Mary and the Saints, poplars
wait for us like sentinels, where
a soprano voice serenades the autumn air
and a boy of five or six appears,
crying out, 'that's my mummy' and
so we stay of course to hear this Grace
sing, hand resting on her boy's small head,
this motet, *Nulla in Mundo,*
– in this world, no honest peace
is free from bitterness, this voice
that lifts and carries us

Later in the village hall
over tea and homemade
double sponge, I do recall
my father and his wallet, with
the photo of his widowed mum,
kept until the end
        – sons and their mothers

Ekaterinburg

from the letters of Grand Duchess Maria Nikolaevna, aged 19

The house is built on a slope
the water here is very good
in the bathtub the water looks light blue
yesterday, like every day
we went for a walk till teatime
the sun was very warm
it penetrated the windows of the second floor

I write to you in semi-darkness
the windows have been whitewashed
the white colour is unpleasant
it's bad for Mama's headaches

Today seems colder
but the thermometer is indecipherable
if you want to write to me
my address is Ekaterinburg,
the Regional Committee, To the chairman,
to be given to me
we don't think they will send us
to another place

Glenside Hospital, 1956

for Eulalie

Admitted

- obese, grey-haired woman
- lays quietly in bed
- active in head & eyes
- refused to cooperate
- signs of religious hysteria

Patient

- motionless in a chair
- cannot name current year
- may be delusional
- recommended massive Largactil therapy & observation

Patient

- dejected & perplexed
- refuses further examination
- recommended daily ECT sessions
- little improvement
- apparent psychotic state
- recommended transfer under Section 37 of Mental Defectives Act

Patient

- says she hears voices & prophecies
- examined stout, middle-aged woman,
- mildly drowsy from Largactil
- speech rambling

Patient

    – fat, hypertensive spinster
    – refuses to respond unless addressed as God

Provisional Diagnosis: Paraphrenic psychosis

'I am God, the Fully Declared in the world
since a child
in the body of a woman
that's why they persecute me
– I go through the stratosphere
into the New Era.'

Now Wake the Prowling Tigers

after reading 'Now Sleeps the Crimson Petal' by Alfred Lord Tennyson

Now let me speak to you
        of love,
the weight of it,
of loves erased
        where does it go, the love
of men, thrown
from the height of towers
        and stoned?
those stamped with
triangled shame
        then gassed?

Where are these men whose
vengeance terriers at our heels?
Wake now; gather up your short lives
put on the skins of
        prowling tigers
with fangs of knives,
face a love that could be death
        in masquerade,
glide now in meteor-burst
leave shining furrows where
your lives might have been,
fold yourselves at last, my dears
and be lost in immortality

Installations

Installation: A form of art, which involves the creation of an enveloping aesthetic or sensory experience in a particular environment, often inviting active engagement or immersion by the spectator.

what the boys are doing in Chaturbate
might surprise their mothers
their range of intimacies bar-coded
for a global market checkout

– nonchalant exhibitionists

#cock flash #flexbiceps #nippleplay #assflash

these boys need your dollars and your adoration
and might decide to talk to you
just keep on tipping
if you like what you see

– a globalisation

of the hard-on although it doesn't rate
so high in the Economic Complexity Index

– solitary boys

DIY
withholding their ejaculations
to boost the Competitive Market
Equilibrium Risk Load

– is this what Adam Smith had in mind

Gross Domestic Product and
will it save us from Recession?

– how many million viewers does it take?

you #beautynthebeast #selfsuckbro #peterbeater
#vanillaguerilla #hunghulk #megahorse

you stand outside
yourself attentive to the lens
watching yourselves watched
this double mirror of Narcissus
traps you in these screens, these cells
of meditation, like monks devoted to
small prayers and genuflections
bodies on display willing to be
pierced with the arrows of our eyes' desires

but dear boys, better
this articulation of your limbs, these installations,
than you carve despair and loneliness
upon your blue-veined wrists
or slip a noose around your necks
in locked garages while the family shops at Safeway

Hey Bro, posting your hard-ons on Twitter won't stop Global Warming

1

come watch me on onlyfans.dot.com   would you   would you
do you like this   did you see this   did you   did you
     am I too sexy   am I   am I
do you want more of this   do you   do you
you can watch the full video here   so watch it
compare my size to yours   am i a god   am i
i'm too hung to be forgotten   aren't I   aren't i
retweet for big   for well hung
here's my god of girth
can you take all this   can you   can you

2

come watch these longer wetter summers as they unfurl
do you like this loss of species   do you   do you
did you see them clearing land   the loss of trees
do you want more of this   do you   do you
did you watch green turtles now in danger   losing habitat
    did you   did you
did you watch the decline in bogong moths   did you   would you
are the jarrah forests still standing   are they   are they
compare the size of kelp forest over all these years
is yours as big as mine   is it   is it
do you want more of this   do you   do you
you can watch the full video here on rising seas   so watch it
retweet for summer bushfires
do you like this   do you   do you
can you take all this   can you   can you
am I a god that i could change all this   am i   am i
do you want more of this   do you   do you

3

when Echo's voice was redacted
        by Zeus' jealous spouse
she wandered until sighting this hunting boy
by name Narcissus   more
beautiful of all online   but alas
rebuffed by this boy so infatuated
by his own reflection, Echo withered
        her voice alone remained
Narcissus in longing for himself so
squandered time and wasted
until the lonely voice of Echo calling
was all that did remain on earth

Go Firmly

after 'The God Abandons Antony' by C.P. Cavafy

your funeral was not meant to be
                an entertainment
when I saw your coffin live-streaming
                down the aisle
I wanted to change the channel
I wanted to change what you'd meant
                to me too

of course, there are tears for
                what is lost
but why weep for what has never been?
                – that's merely petulance
there were letters left forgotten
                – calls unanswered
our lives barely nudging against each other
                then moving on

after the service I walked on the beach
seaweed towered above me like
                uninhabitable high-rise
and I was small again
so go now firmly to the window
and weep your paltry tears
                of farewell

That Hereness/Thereness Thing

After school the boy
sits on the fence
staring down the street
within the rivers of his mind
thinking of the thereness beyond
the hereness of this small town

When the father's car tops
Callington Hill, the Adelaide Plains
laid out like his mother's
picnic blanket
every thereness seems
possible to the boy

That long road from boarding school
pours away from the boy
like lava flow, carrying
his parents back
to the country
thereness now impossible

Outside the boy-man's house
in the mountains of the Philippines
a man from further up the mountain,
stops to ask
'where does that road go to?'
had the boy-man reached
the limits of his thereness?

The boy-now-older man
scans the view from his nested balcony
discovers at last
that the thereness thing
was living there within
and is boundless

The Taste of the Wolf

with a furtive touch of lips by love wounded
a man will often kiss as if licking honey
I heard thunder when the fly hit the window
then the echo in the Amazon forests

a man will often kiss as if licking honey
the snake lurk behind fragrant flowers
was there an echo in the Amazon forest
the night we first kissed

does a snake lurk behind fragrant flowers
the air undulating with dragonflies
the night that we first kissed
when every sense was electrified?

the air undulated with dragonflies
like the taste in the mouth of the wolf
when every sense was electrified
land charged by wind and deceit

did you taste the mouth of the wolf
wash your hair in low-dwelling clouds
in land charged by wind and deceit
with just a furtive touch of lips wounded by love

Those Vows of Silence

for Paddy S

When the heat of summer
cracks open the sky, bleeding

betrayal, green-striped burrowing
frogs go subterranean

those Cistercians of the mudflats
cocoon themselves in robes of silence

with vows now eons old, preserving
contemplation in this state of aestivation.

What of your involuntary retreat
to the hidden corridors and corners

of your cerebellum, remembering
days when we were on fire with

dreams that so unseated us, how we
journeyed where the mountains sang

siren songs, how love bewitched
us then with words like incantations

to gods newly met, so do
you still hear the cloistered

echo of those psalms
we sang as one?

Outside IGA

Outside IGA the beanied
man's guitar riffs 'Stairway
to Heaven', each note ascending
to the tops of trees, arrowing into
that impossible blue

Down on the beach a father
and his small son stand
hand-in-hand, sculpted
from the thin air of expectation
gazing towards the puzzling ocean

I walk towards my waiting friend
– I know behind her mask
she's smiling

We're all just lighting candles
at the Shrine of the
Madre de la Esperanza

Ballast

in Stingray Bay, half-
buried in sand
this shipwrecked ballast-stone

if I place my fingers here
in these indents of memory, I
feel the steel-shod strike of

chisel run up the stonemason's
arm in some 1800s Dorset quarry
this shock-link spans the seas and years

unites us both in need for more
longtimeness, some solidness to leave behind
but there's just this cornerstone

this beach, the ever-present
ocean and all those boxes of an
unsorted life that will remain

Afternoons

You rise from my bed,
the hesitant light of afternoon
touches the turn of your head,
your smile, the pulse of your chest, the rest
shadowed in want as you leave

I wait for the street lamps' glow
the hum of traffic to dim

Now I pause in the walled
garden of pleasure and the
ossuary of disappointment

Michelangelo's Failure

In 1991 Pierro Cannato
attacked Michelangelo's *David*
with a hammer, ordered (he said)
by its model, Nani of Venice
for a failure to convey
the beauty of this nakedness

so how can words express
this adoration of skin
that made a jealous god, alarmed
by unexpected confluence of lust
and grace, to banish Eden's naked pair
both more beautiful and dangerous
than he who made them

who knew when earth was void
that dust would shape into
this symphony of limbs in motion
this machine god-crafted, pistoned
with rebellion, so full of
treachery in its perfection, too
prone to sin for
any god to sanction

yet, as years advance, betrayed
by scars and disappointments, this
naked beauty, transfigures, miraculous,
into an altered, mystic temple
far beyond some Michelangelo's imagine
      a wielded chisel or even
      what the god intended

To Be Wild

after 'Born To be Wild' (Steppenwolf)

sometimes all I want is
to ride
pillion on a
Harley-Davidson Sportster
with a shirtless Chris
Hemsworth along the Great
Ocean Road, tightening my thighs
on those dangerous corners, stopping
at secluded beaches for swimming
in Speedos, then watching
the sun go down at Port Campbell
between his muscular thighs,
him riding pillion
home in the dark so I can
feel his three-day stubble
rasp the back of my neck

Passer, deliciae

after Catullus

Red dog, pet of my crush
with whom he often plays, holding
you in his lap or giving you
morsels to taste and to bite
provoking you to lick his face
        – whenever he, the source of all my
thoughts has a mind for some
other kind of play, he may
taunt me at last and play
with me instead of you,
let me too lie between those
legs outstretched and loosen
all hidden and secret parts
of you

This Corner

here in this corner where
cabbage whites skitter, then

doze in the blue repose of
lavender, pale-flecked garden

skinks assemble for consultations
lilies red as harlot lips resist

all winds, hydrangea with bobbin lace
heads seek eucalyptus shade

water drops fly up from
wings of blue wrens, *asperges me*

is this the terminus of all
my longings here in this sanctuary

at whose vestibule I hesitate
expecting both the comfort of holy

waters and the anxiety of snakes?

The Carnage of Petals

title from a poem from *Look* by Solmaz Sharif

These red poppies
rise like slaughtered soldiers
distracted by the tasks of resurrection,
heads so heavy with the memory
of blood & retribution from
fields of Fromelle, the Somme and more

Despite the buffeting of winds
they soar on stilts, stalks
as unreliable as promises cut short,
remorseless, persistent, towering
now like *moko jumbie*, those
healer spirits, seeking out
the spaces in-between innocence
and excommunication, between the gaps in garden
storms, stained with wounded poppy petals
while we, with our casual, glittering knives,
still slit the throats of
our enemies' children

Full-throated

God is just a word

a woman felled by
the sharp axe of childbirth

men in hospital wards
weighed down by the succubus of pain

adolescent boys in vests of suicide
briefly defiant before exploding in surprise

the shocking ecstasies of sex's hot release
in the curtained heart of afternoons

blackbirds sheltering in Moonah thicket
wide-eyed falcons circling

the morning lily opening wide
her throat for arias of turquoise

God is just some words
        like these

The Elastic Horizon

for Chris V

You gave me Sibelius
'this polonaise for bears'
violin bows slicing
up the hills of foggy,
notes going bonkers skimming
over seas of pink camellia,
azalea, rhododendron,
so unlike the dusty
paddocks of my boyhood

You gave me feet
that felt the trembling
of a timber deck riding
river currents, propelling
me towards that elastic
horizon, always stretching
into the Could Be Possibles

        – your unstoppable gift

Falling

I fall
in love too
easily

– with tattooed
men on building sites
in hard hats and steel-
capped boots who refrain
from whistling when I walk
past, I yearn to fashion with
them tiny origami swans to
set afloat from riverbanks
buzzing with blue
salvia & cabbage whites

– with the smiles of
young men stacking shelves in
supermarkets, or at checkouts
asking me how my day's been so far,
I want to read them the love poems of Ovid
or perhaps the Song of Songs as they
gaze at me dreamily amidst
the cans of diced tomatoes and
those mushrooms with the texture
of moist lips

– with tanned tradesmen in shorts and
inverted caps who nod at me in
deserted car parks, imagine
us together on a silver beach
lying in each other's arms as I
point out the journeyings of
constellations, then waking to the crooning
gulls, swimming naked in a sea like tepid
tea, feeling the current bear
us towards the triumph of the Deep Blue Black

– falling is too easy

To Have Some Weight

after 'What the Finch Knows', Kevin Brophy

the pelican understands
the meaning of
avoirdupois
how to balance loss with
hope ascending from the
surfaces of summer, rising
casually through the sinewy
ether wings forged of steel
and whimsy wind-stroked
victor over gravity's desires

how can we attain that
lifting up into the space of
weightlessness in air fashioned
from impossibles where we are
mere imposters?

A Box of Photos

without this box of photos
faded, wrinkled, worn

how could I recall the years' acceleration
of signposts blurring past?

my early arm around my grandma's neck
her hat of straw and flowers, askance

– till now my selfied face
with greying hair and skin like hers

many moments exposed to light and time
revealed by whim and wish and love

so what of the unrecorded
mislaid round corners of memories fickle

and all those hands that held the camera too
slipped away down other paths and roads?

no wonder how we clutch these pasts,
precious jewels, fleeing lives
consumed by fire and love

living with erasures

in Ely Cathedral saints
wear apostasy on shattered

faces oblivious to millennial men
muscle-flexing online, a tsunami

of selfies, desperate for followers
or likes, overhung with

awesomeness, does my cock
look big in this, identified by

pixellated genitals, body-true
coming down in codpiece uncertainty

        in the wetlands I record the
        songs of growling grass frogs

        in preparation for
        the Extinction,
        the erasures of
        our names

investigate

in order to investigate
the human heart, put on

wings of the wedge-tailed eagle
soar above everdayness   conceal

yourself in the wind as smoke
does   linger in the underheart

of waves   ponder the messages
moving grasses write in sand

be seduced by the legs of
ladybirds on skin   cocoon yourself

in parcels of laughter (loosely), in bliss,
all this fine ejaculate of an intoxicated creator

pilgrimages of the short-finned eel

travel west across a basalt
plain, past stony rises, shallow
lakes, woodlandsgrasslands, all
    the scourscar left
    from earthskin ruptures
    the thrust of fire aloft
    tracks of damaged veins

here are penitents
    shot-through with
wattle-gold and green, the
    short-finned eels, on pilgrimages
and penances, contrition-bent
    for massacres' elisions, the
lacrimae of Tarerer, the
    Maar volcano in childbirth

now we tip, we stagger into
    where we've been, remembering
the tremble-tremble, the Great Shuddering
    the soft flight of flat stones
across water, eels migrating to
    the Coral Sea to spawn

Latitude 38 South

though body-bolted to
soil, I may yet soar into

air fashioned from impossibles
along latitude 38 south

to Mar del Plata and the
great shearwater   heavy with

travel   bearing a private hope of
one white egg   needling its stiff

straight wings with littoral ambitions
in the scritch and stretch sky

knitting up the latitudes
crammed with a planet's litanies

of lurch and rustle
        this is how we connect

languages of hands

the night I first kissed you
I drove home through darkened Adelaide
past the church where a mitred bishop had
smeared my hands with godly – stamped,
sacred, *a priest forever*

that day the dialect my body spoke
was untranslatable, only now
was I learning the declensions of desire,
the grammar of arousal,
calling on anonymous night
to touch the unmarked parts of me

my god-filled hands still scorched
from holding you, words & wounds
forging stigmatas, the pressure
of your lips was a seedling
pressed into damp earth and watered

only then did night become
my friend with its darkenings,
enfolding angels' wings,
the tremors, ebbs and flows
into the beating heart
of a god reckless

The Calling

The late afternoons, the smell of rain in the air, riding home from the mountains through the barrios. I feel the itch of dried sweat in my armpits and lower back, passing storefronts where drying fish flaps in the sun, women in bright-coloured dresses fan themselves in the shade with banana leaves. Groups of young men, grimy from cutting coconut all day, are gathering to drink.

Hey compadre they call as we pass, invite us to stop and try the local fermenting coconut wine. My stomach lurches recalling its bitter, sharp taste, but I'm seduced by this loud, friendly invitation. I'm the only white man for hundreds of kilometres. My longing for acceptance overrides everything.

here on the open road, my thighs begin
to shape a different sort of god
more Lover than Father

A DNA test

1. for best results

from saliva, swab
for cheek cells, rotating
to trap clues from
accidents of time, percolated,
desiccated, refined, reduced

2. taken from toppled buildings

in Gaza where all the anger
of the universe is leaking out,
families scrabbling for the failing
breath of children with names louder
than the screams of those hysterical shells
rising – rejected prayers

3. from Moroccan boys swimming

towards El Tarajal, replenishing
the oceans with salty tears,
oh if only sea knew how
to shape footprints, they might
yet reclaim their homes

4. all that comes from

our bodies, this spit, this rage,
this breath, these tears bleeding
from bodies on beaches
not their own

5. expect algorithms to

generate your *Ethnicity Estimate,*
this guilty heritage, to be
as furious as you feel

Nevinbumbaan Returns

the women in black are
on the trains, walking, crawling
carrying hurt and placards,
they're tearing down the
wounded sky, riding the river
of steel and glittering revenge
knitting up the sky again with
skeins of blood and afterbirth

the women in black are bearing aloft
women dumped in parks and laneways,
abandoned in kitchens and shallow graves
reanimating an angry, ghostly army

men are hiding behind their
phallic masks and important meetings
their secret business, initiation
rites and cases of defamation
worried they'll be consumed by
Nevinbumbaan, the cannibal goddess

       – the women are marching

these bodies of men

                tentative at first
programmed for punch, choke, kill, with

veins of excess bulge, hands of confusion
whether to catch the fall of small

birds or crush their bones, their arms
are clubs, testosterone prickling under marbled

skin, tender killers concealed in shapes
wrought of rose-water and the blue

of iris, legs rooted in some
orcharded trees, warm here where

hand rests on exposed neck
dismayed by the thrum and throb of

kisses' thump of thuds' soft bite, this
yearning to measure the long length or

smell, the perfume
of my hair

Still 'Falling'

after reading 'For the Fallen' by Laurence Binyon

shout out, we're
coming home again but
not this time enclosed in
boxes draped in flags
well-rinsed in holy, lifted
triumphant, solemn-shouldered
returning to the wombs of C-17s

not in time for Anzac Day, alas
when disembodied faces taste
the candled dawn, those serried
ranks of angels reprising worn-out
wails of grief

not in time for men who hide
in rooms with blinds pulled down,
their minds on safety-catch release for
*at the going down of the sun and in
the morning* no one remembers them

who tallies up the stats, the
glory/safety ratio that feeds
future leaders' recycled words?

permit these men grow old, *as we
that are left grow old*, rebirth
not those youthful ghosts of
a nationhood's forever wars, for
to the end, to the end,
their deaths are
       – war's duplicity

All the Deep Pulse

so this is why we live to
feel the deep, hot pulse and smell
what lies between heaven's blue
caress and dung's sharp shock

to weep the winking wet of
inner streets, trawling
for discarded kisses, demanding
nights must tell us who we truly are

to await the whorl of
light that may bubble up from
buried deep, sprinkle me with
hyssop, whiten me like snow

this always anticipating men
the chrysalis splitting, the
slow unfolding of seducer-wings
in bedrooms above the Bay

here in this valley of hot, love
comes dipped in amnesia,
inhibitions fall away as
discarded snakeskins do

where small wrens reign, an
agile creator's afterthoughts
this cracking of the shell,
this queering of my blood,

I do proclaim as beautiful

ice creams and AK47s

1.

the Taliban are holding
melting ice creams and
AK47s   not smiling
how many Taliban can you fit
in a dodgem car
> this is not a riddle
> & this is not a rehearsal

2.

Body Parts Found
in Landing Gear of
C-17 cargo plane
From Kabul,
Officials Say

3.

I saw you in the dusty stampede
a child by each hand,
your wife beside you
(not behind you)
my arms ached
to cross the miles of
hard red desert and scale
the teeth of mountains
but my arms are weak, still I
ached to hold you in my heart and will,
one day to meet
your daughter the doctor
on my regular
suburban check-up, explain
my rising blood   pressure

open waters

for Mary O'Connor

       my grandmother
left home in a hurry

bequeathing us a gift, the
restlessness of open waters, this

ache to find safe harbour
she carried, memory's weight of

men slitting their throats with
rusty scythes beside their disbelieving

cows, we the true amphibians
professional mongrels all, scouring

the wreckages of rubble for chromosomes
enough to sculpt a better shape of us

so what am I to do with
this ruin of myself, except

observe how late light of afternoons
bends through tea tree, breathes

air, she might mistake for sea spray
thrown up from Clare's Cliffs of Moher

In No Particular Order

        today
Kabul capitulated to the Taliban
solemn men shoulder AK47s taking selfies
around a president's abandoned desk
        – a thousand sharp knives unsheathed

on the walking path
discarded plastic package
for a dildo size XL
price $44.95

a kangaroo bounding across
the road in front of me, I
brake suddenly, he disappears,

curfew begins tonight at 9 p.m.
playgrounds will be closed
Operation Stay at Home begins
        I break slowly

on the back track I record
the sounds of spotted marsh frogs,
the common eastern froglet
*breeds during spring to autumn, but
also in winter after heavy rain*

the beast of events upon us
        each breath an experiment

the road to Ronda

Make yourself a clean soft bed
to rest in my heart's shrine
So that I never forget you.
– from *Praeter rerum seriem* by Josquin Desprez (1450–1521)

on the road to Ronda lie
the unquiet bones of mothers, daughters, sons
the inconvenienced bones of children
ulnas, fibulas, femurs, discomfrontled all
surprised by sudden dislocations
from neighbourly clubs and swords

on the train to Ronda we
gaze at slipstreamed silver olive groves
red soils as if wind-blown from some Saharas

in Ruedo Doña Elvira, the Virgin de la Paz
holds vigils over old Moro streets
where ringing steps of rabid mobs
are barely fading

on El Puento Nevo tourists pose
for selfies, deaf to echoed prayers
of Los Musacrados still
plunging down the years

in Plaza Duquesa de Parcent we
feast on *espetos,* tomatoes, drink
Albarino as the average dead pass by
like lengthening Shades of nearby
almond trees, stronger than we
the living, anticipating their
state of knowingness *beyond
the order of this world*

westerlies

irritable winds of summer shred
petticoated petals of lilies / dishabille
expose the throbbing shame of stamens

ravens in confusion surge for
conifer conferencing / seagulls challenge
resolute westerlies / witnesses against

a glaucos sky / a blackbird's
song after rain / the splayed
and naked limbs of men in

dunes like discarded ambitions
the sun intent on desiccating dreams

oh beauty's sweet and many an ambush

Waiting

                when
we carry our children to
your borders / you offer us

razor wire to wrap them in
against the cold / why are stones

upon the beaches of our shipwrecks
mere replicas of fossilled tears

pressured by the years of
seeking refuge / we must await the

uncertainty of the sacred light
of miracles that snatches us up

then throws us to our knees
worshipping / the approaching

storms are merely preludes to your
rumbling arguments of disputed borders

Rioting on the Equinox

banners & placards shout Freedom
        freedom to curse
the light for
        its casual revelations
        freedom to roam
like sheep that
have gone astray
        to piss
upon the dreams
of slaughtered men
        in
        shrines of remembering

so across this bridge of days
lurks a hollowed-out light
picking over the shattered
glass of streets
a day when sun
apportions out
this impartial
where the cut & paste
the haste
of swallows is knitting up
all the available light

sunflowers need full sunshine

for Ukraine

when missiles cracked open the ribs
of sleeping Kyiv   children carried their colouring
books down into basements
sunlight was betrayed

when bedrooms exploded unexpectedly
like party balloons, then   sunlight
was betrayed

when blood stained the snow
around Santa Sophia   wisdom
was betrayed

when trains filled with fleeing families,
carrying cats and dogs   sunlight
was betrayed

in Lviv cathedral when men in bomber jackets
and beanies bore Christ Crucified underground
reverently as if newly dead
to wait out the resurrection

only then do we command you, the invading
soldiers, 'place these sunflower seeds
in your pockets so flowers will bloom
when you die and are buried in our soil'

Waiting for light

light shines where it will
        strategically
it creeps across gibbered plains

lifts lorikeets into
their clear blue song

sketches the philosophies
of lugworms on deserted beaches

even craters of the moon must
wait in line for its approval

each star suspended in
hope of light's anointing

we too must wait as
the great egret does
that sentinel becalmed

time-painted on the shallows
of the wetlands she bends the light to
spear unwary prey

while lovelight blocks
the light of ancient stars
simmering on the edge of sight

Let the bright Seraphim

after hearing 'Da ya think I'm sexy?' by Rob Stewart) and 'Let the bright Seraphim' from Handel's *Samson*

that summer
wore tight jeans &
white T-shirts

we were everywhere
salt dreams on our skin
the air redolent of coconut oil

under mosquito nets
in our underwear we moved
like saints in ecstasy
to the distant beat of
of 'Da ya think I'm sexy?'

but the sun was aging
the moon hurling its cratered
shadows on us, lesions
that blossomed on our skin
became Kaposi's sarcoma

If you want my body
and you think I'm sexy
is it enough to give thanks
that we have survived to
give witness to all these things?

no, let the bright Seraphim
be loud, uplifted, let
angel trumpets blow
to avenge this failure
of our flesh endangered

Arias of Longing

In this garden lilies fecund
on slender green are arching
aching for ascension with
longings that have some limits

Why within us is this throbbing
to be the high   the frack
held back
 by roots
 of interior preoccupations
 by shame's incessant chatter

This weight of rhythmic want
our burden
oh the beauty and the broodle

The symphony of hearts' castrati
does linger

Communion

'There you go brother'
he said
handing me a coffee
but of course I thought
of you my brother &
how we were as children

on nights at home when
the gentle tide-tug of words
and jokes between us flowed
until one voice went silent dragged
into the undertow of dreaming

for growing up in the shade
of saints and angels, did we not
press their faces between
the pages of our prayerbooks,
like rare exotic flowers

I'm a child again talking
into darkness expecting
some reply but all I hear
is the rustling answer of the
khirqah, that long white skirt of a
whirling dervish, tugging at my heart
now so full of a life's centripetal desires

Sing Out for Ukraine

for Yuri Kerpatenko, Ukrainian orchestra conductor, murdered in the occupied city of Kherson over his refusal to participate in a concert put on by Russian authorities

In October
the plane-tree buds
burst pale green while
along the creek the ranks
of yellow Iris stand guard

In Mary of the Angels
the black-clad choir sings siren songs
to seduce the hearts of tyrants

Do not mistake the organ's trembling
groan for a missile's deadly aria
or the sopranos' high notes
for the widows' ululations

So I will light a candle
against the sun   quietly*
while all around me war
bullies   loudly

Fathers of Ukraine
as our foes press on from every side*
hold your children closer
so that they may live

Who else will carry flowers and prayers
to your own well-kept gravesites

* Italicised lines quoted from lyrics of music at concert *Sing Out for Ukraine* at St Mary's Basilica, Geelong on 15 October 2022.

shall be changed

'In a moment, in the twinkling of an eye…for the trumpet shall sound, and the dead shall be raised incorruptible, and we shall be changed.' – 1 Corinthians 15:52

the wise raven is hauling sticks
long day back and forth – preparing
slicing the ambitious air
to build afresh

as tectonic plates of conflict
shift and grind – all those equipments
of war spew shrapnel over
kindergartens
as the oh so solid dunes retreat
before the ocean's ululations
and blood-red skies
replete with signs and wonders

have their own secret
strategies
our eyes are fixed on gods and
earth torn up and burning   and so

we must pay close attention to each small breeze   to
each new portent like
the night sky slashed with silk
the hands of my grandfather's clock

accelerating   for here
in the Great In-Between we swing

      days stretch the light to lean
lazily into the shaded corners
of our unconscious where
we yearn to touch
all those incorruptibles

we are all changed

Anthem for a Redeeming Youth

after reading 'Anthem for a Doomed Youth' by Wilfred Owen

what clarion voice is this
that shimmers in the
stained-glass-windowed Jesus
of St Paul's, 'imbued with grace
true and beautiful' singing
do not fear to put
thy naked feet into the river
sweet, a voice unloosening all
our hearts' tight knots

in the ruins of her home
where missiles rain like
unanswered prayers
the violinist crafts her
elegies of love that promise
'not a wave shall trouble thee', so

oh all you young women
and men sing us your new songs,
that startle and disturb us
then stitch up again our
scattered selves
with hope's fine threads for

only you the young
can withstand the rigours
of a duty such as this

after all kinds of walking around

    1. in morning's dunecreep canopy
in purpled pigface
sea sandwort, saltwort

and marram grass, I met
the wallaby there in
the crackling air we

stared
under skeins of cloud
and sunlight unravelling

cloud-backed shadows spiralling
kadoodling turtle doves uplifting
into shape-shifting air

    2. to pay attention is to hear
divine voices below our feet
where blind fish sing glory songs

these times do have the mind of past winters
so listen to warnings of ageing *hibakusha*
about bodies corroborating scarred indifference

scrutinise the world intently for
are we not here to touch these earthly things
with our caressing words

to listen to the earth
its beating heart
find fine words to

reconsecrate all
the scribbles jottings
sketchings of a universe

Acknowlegements

Poems in this collection have previously appeared in *Melbourne Writers Lockdown Anthology, London Grip, Poetry Wivenhoe* (UK), *Blue Nib* (Ireland), *Blue Pepper, Poetry on the Move* (University of Canberra), *Bent Street* 4.2 – 2020, *Eunoia Review* (Singapore), *Melbourne Culture Corner, Unusual Work, Right Now, Queerlings* (UK), *Meniscus* literary journal, *Impossible Archetype* (Ireland), *Verandah, The Lake* (UK), *Adirondak Review(*US), *Right Now, Brushstrokes II, The Crow, Sheila-Na-Gig* (US), *Cerasus Magazine* (UK), *Communion Magazine, Confluence Magazine* (US), *Last Leaves* (US), *Discretionary Love*(US), *Eureka Street and The Bond Street Review* (US).

Poems have also been included in recent Australian anthologies including *Poetry for the Planet*, the Ros Spencer Poetry Contest Anthology (2020–21), *fourWthirty-two* New Writing 2021, *Milestones* (Ginninderra Press) and longlisted in the Liquid Amber Poetry prize 2022 and 2023.

Thanks to members of the small poetry group, especially Yvonne Adami, Wendy Fleming, Lyn Chatham, Geraldine Moyle, Kathryn Ross, Rosemary Blake, Julie Maclean and members of the U3A poetry class. Thanks also to Anthony Ash for scientific information on the nuclear physics behind the Excitation of Entanglement process.

Special thanks to Julie Maclean for her constant encouragement and editorial advice and, as always, to Stephen for wisdom on the use of the pluperfect.

About the author

John Bartlett's first poetry chapbook *The Arms of Men* was published by Melbourne Poets Union in 2019 and a second chapbook, *Songs of the Godforsaken*, in 2020 by Picaro Poets. His full poetry collection, *Awake at 3 a.m.*, was released by Ginninderra Press in 2020. He was the winner of the 2020 Ada Cambridge Poetry Prize. He is also the author of three novels, *Towards a Distant Sea*, *Estuary* and *Jack Ferryman: Reluctant Private Investigator*. He has also published a collection of short stories, *All Mortal Flesh,* and a collection of his published non-fiction, *A Tiny and Brilliant Light*. He writes on unceded Wadawurrung country.

www.ingramcontent.com/pod-product-compliance
Lightning Source LLC
Chambersburg PA
CBHW070118110526
44587CB00015BA/2362